Il le promet, croyez-le ... fût-ce un jour.

ne mourrait—? la ... mour

Avec ses feux je peignais ses douleurs:

Que cette image en paraît moins charmante.

au milieu de mes larmes, C'était l'amou

le ciel ... qu'avec lui j'ai perdu.

Il brûle tout, ce doux empoisonneur.

Demandez-donc s'il donne le bonheur:

De gré, de force, amour sera le maître;

Vous souffrirez, ou vous ferez souffrir.

Dès qu'il revient, on tremble nuit et jou

cependant....oui, l'amour rend heureuse!

Vous demandez si l'amour rend heureuse

Ah! pour un jour d'existence amoureuse,

Quand je vivais tendre et craintive ama

Sur son portrait j'ai versé tant de pleurs,

i le sourire, éclair inattendu, Brille parf

c'était lui, mais sans armes; C'éta

Sans lui, le cœur est un foyer sans fla

J'ai dit bien vrai comme il déchire une â

Vous le saurez: oui, quoi qu'il en puisse

Et, dans sa fièvre alors lente à guéri

Dès qu'on l'a vu, son absence est affreu

Souvent enfin la mort est dans l'amour

dedicated to:

celebrating
Love
share, remember, cherish

JIM McCANN, FOUNDER

**Andrews McMeel
Publishing, LLC**
Kansas City · Sydney · London

For information, write Andrews McMeel Publishing, LLC, an Andrews McMeel Universal company,
1130 Walnut Street, Kansas City, Missouri 64106

ISBN-13: 978-1-4494-0262-4

Library of Congress Control Number: 2010931442

11 12 13 14 15 SMA 10 9 8 7 6 5 4 3 2 1

www.andrewsmcmeel.com

ATTENTION: SCHOOLS AND BUSINESSES

Andrews McMeel books are available at quantity discounts with bulk purchase for educational,
business, or sales promotional use. For information, please write to: Special Sales Department,
Andrews McMeel Publishing, LLC, 1130 Walnut Street, Kansas City, Missouri 64106.

Project Manager and Editor: Heidi Tyline King

Designed by Alexis Siroc

Produced by SMALLWOOD & STEWART, NEW YORK CITY

Illustration credit information on page 70.

introduction

During good times or challenging times, having the love of friends and family is a powerful advantage in life and business. I know this firsthand because ours is a family-run business and the contributions from my siblings and extended family have not only helped our business succeed, they've also helped keep me sane (mostly!). I was thinking about these relationships not too long ago after our annual McCann family weekend at our beach house on Long Island. My wife, Marylou, and I were sitting in our favorite lounge chairs drinking a glass of wine and watching a magnificent golden sunset slip over the bay. Our children and their families had just packed up and left. For the first time in five years, they were all living close by in the New York area, and all were healthy, happy, and doing well. As for the two of us, we were celebrating 37 years of marriage. Marveling at how blessed we were, it suddenly hit us: At this moment, this one moment, our life felt just about perfect.

In the springtime of our marriage, we were just a couple of kids, young and in love but with no idea about what life was really like. During those years of babies and tight budgets, I was working two jobs and struggling to make a go of my florist shops. But Marylou rarely complained, even when I came up with the cockamamie idea of round-the-clock customer service, 24 hours a day, seven days a week—and forgot to tell her that she and I were the customer service representatives. I knew it was true love when my wife, between nightly feedings for the baby, would answer telephone calls from customers cheerfully at three a.m. and still manage to smile at me in the morning!

Later, like everyone else, we muddled through our share of troubles: job demands, teenagers, family issues, the passing of our parents . . . but somehow, we managed. We figured out how to charge our batteries when the times were good so that when the tough times rolled around, we had enough juice to make it through. We discovered that love, like life, wasn't always fair. There were times when Marylou needed my strength to get her through—and a whole lot of times when I relied on her to share the weight of my burdens.

We also learned that love is a lot more than romantic dinners and family get-togethers. In real, lasting love, there is a familiarity and depth of relationship created over time. Whether marriage or friendship, it's the feeling that somebody's "got your back"—the same somebody who knows all your bad habits but loves you anyway, and who tells you what you don't want to hear even when you know it's the truth.

All of our yesterdays—both good and bad—had led us to this moment. We realized what a gift it was to grow old together through the fall and winter seasons of our love. But we were surprised at how sweet it was to have the chance to observe our children as they passed through the seasons of love in their lives. That weekend, we watched our daughter with her new baby and grew teary-eyed by how tender and caring a mother she was, an affirmation that maybe we did some things right. We were overwhelmed by the peace we felt from having our oldest son, James, move back from the Midwest to within a few miles of our house. And we were giddy knowing that within the year, our youngest son, Matt, and his fiancée, Jen, would tie the knot and begin the journey that we had started so long ago.

This is my love story, but you'll find that its underlying message is not so different from many of those shared in this book by Celebrations.com and 1-800-FLOWERS.com customers. That's because at the end of the day, we're all striving for the same thing. Like air, water, and food, one of our most basic needs is having people we care about and who care about us. Love is the ultimate connection.

one

spring

Every wish I've ever wished . . .
Every hope I've ever had . . .
Every dream I've ever dreamed
Came true the day I met you!

*I prayed every night for God to bless me
with someone special. He answered my prayer
when he sent me you.*

I love you more than there are stars in the sky.

—RACHEL A.

In 1959, on my 12th birthday, I found the love of my life. I had gone to a dance class; he was dancing with another girl. Our eyes locked, my heart skipped a few beats, and I felt weak at the knees (yes, it does happen!). Three years later, we ended up at the same birthday party, and it happened again. Soon after we were dating, and we married when I was 19. Our so-called "puppy love" is now going on 43 years! —JANE S.

If love is blind, why is lingerie so popular?

Finding you was luckier than waking up in a
field of four-leaf clovers.

I don't need electricity.
You are the light of my life.

In my darkest moment I found my brightest light.
I am so glad I found you.

Somewhere along the way
I must have done something right. I know this
because I have you in my life!

Love that is not madness is not love.

—PEDRO CALDERÓN DE LA BARCA

*My heart swells as I look his way;
Does he know that his smile
has made my day?*

—ELLEN R.

spring

LET'S GET PHYSICAL...

✳ Being in love produces the same physiological responses as fear: pupil dilation, sweaty palms, and increased heart rate.

✳ Men who kiss their wives each morning live five years longer than those who don't.

✳ Medical experts suggest you are more likely to catch a common cold by shaking hands than by kissing.

✳ Love and marriage are boosts for your health, so much so that one doctor admitted that if a new drug had the same impact, virtually every doctor in the country would be recommending it.

spring

*A*fter a few months of dating, I knew that Tammy was the one I wanted to marry. But having lived through my parents' divorce, I was in no rush to tie the knot. One night when we went out with friends, they badgered me for almost an hour about when I was going to pop the question, I finally replied that I wasn't ready . . . and that I might not ever be. Understandably, this was quite a shock to Tammy. The drive home was filled with uneasy silence.

The next morning, I read in the Bible about a man who prayed: The woman who brings him water will be the one he brings back for his master to marry. If it worked for him, I figured it would work for me. So I prayed that if Tammy was supposed to be my wife, then God needed to "provide the diamonds."

That afternoon, we went to a party at the beach. As we were setting up, a man walked by, paused for a few awkward moments, then walked on. None of our friends knew him. Later, he returned, stopping by once again. We made small talk, and I asked him what he did. "I'm a diamond broker," he replied. Then he looked at Tammy and said to me, "You'd better marry this girl before she gets away. Call this number and ask for Jewels. Tell him Wally sent you and he'll take care of your diamond needs."

I felt this was a sign, but still, I confided to a friend that if I was supposed to get married, then God needed to provide the diamonds.

The next day, I went to see Jewels. He showed me an array of loose diamonds, but when he brought out the last one I knew it was "the one"—pear-shaped and perfect. But I just couldn't afford it, and wouldn't be able to for some time.

I was feeling pretty low when my mother called that night and said, "I know how much you like Tammy, so I sent your Nana's ring to you. You can use these two diamonds as you wish."

I was stunned. When I prayed for God to provide the diamonds, I didn't really expect him to provide the diamonds. Once the package arrived, I exchanged my Nana's ring for both Tammy's engagement ring and my wedding ring. —CHRISTOPHER G.

spring

Love at First Sight

According to research, love at first sight is not just a fairy tale. If a person is in the right emotional frame of mind, it can take as little as 30 seconds to fall in love. Physical appearance tops the list for attraction, but a desire to know more about the person is another factor. Interestingly, men fall first but are usually the most fickle, a sign that it is possible to fall in love with more than one person at a time.

Love is . . .
when there is only
one ice pop left and
your brother gives it to you.

—ALISON H.

spring

True love *can show up in the strangest of places. Long before the days of Facebook and Twittering, I met my husband through a social networking phenomenon known as the "party line," where singles could call in and talk to other singles from around the country. One night, a guy sent me a connection request. I denied it, but he kept sending them. Finally, after 50 or more, I accepted. We talked for six hours and continued our conversation over the next two months before deciding to meet. When he got out of the taxi at my house, it hit me—love at first sight. Two months later we were married; this year we celebrate our ten-year anniversary.*

—DANYALE N.

Take it from me—whoever said that good things come to those who wait knew what she was talking about! When I met my lover six years ago through friends, something inside me screamed, "This is it—he is the one!" We were both in relationships, and for the next year, we tried not to act on our feelings, but it soon became so difficult that we decided it was best if we not see each other at all.

Fast-forward six years and he looks me up on Facebook. One quick conversation and I just knew, "This is it—he is the one!" We love the same things, have the same life goals, and there is a connection between us like nothing I have ever known. We missed out on the last six years but have a lifetime—our lifetimes—ahead of us. —KASSANDRA J.

The worst thing you can do for love is deny it; so when you find that special someone, don't let anyone or anything get in your way.

SOMETIMES LOVE MEANS HAVING TO WAIT *for the right time. After tragically losing my first love, I believed I would never find love again. But then "G" came along. I feel complete when I am with him, and I am amazed at how much I care for him. But I am also puzzled that this time around, my love is more mature. There is a reality of being true to myself before giving myself to another. So for the moment, we are staying focused on our individual dreams, knowing in our hearts that one day will be the first day of the rest of our lives.*

—MA-LE A.

spring

IF EMOTIONS WERE OCEANS
I'D TAKE TO THE SEA . . .
BUILD A BIG SAILBOAT
AND TAKE YOU WITH ME.
ADRIFT ON OUR LOVE
WE'D SAIL FAR FROM SHORE,
CAST OFF ALL WORRIES
AND LAUGH EVERMORE.

Isn't it funny that when you are not in love, all those mushy sentiments you hear don't make sense? But then, when you are in love, you can't imagine anything closer to the truth. For me, it's the clichéd airport reunion story.

I was there waiting patiently for my girlfriend to arrive. We had spent nine months and 3,000 miles apart. I had no idea what to expect. Would we still have a connection? Had time cooled our affections?

When the first passengers appeared, my hands were sweating. My heartbeat was so loud I was worried the guy next to me could hear it.

And then . . . I saw her. I'm not kidding—it was as if a single spotlight was shining down on her in the middle of a sea of darkness. Her long blonde hair fell down her back in waves. Her blue eyes were piercing. Her smile lit up the room.

We ran toward each other just like in the movies. I caught her in my arms, spinning us in circles in the middle of the busy terminal. For a second, we were the only ones in the entire airport. Just like that, the doubts and the distance fell away, leaving the two of us together, in love.

—THOMAS W.

spring

I never thought I'd love a younger man, but here I am, a cougar, falling for someone in a way that I've never fallen for anyone else. In honesty, however, it wouldn't work if we were the same age. I had to wait for him to grow up. And now, as an older woman, I have just arrived at a place of confidence and comfort with myself. In this moment, we are the right person for the other. —CHRISTIE M.

I'm not looking for someone who can live with me. I'm looking for someone who can't live without me.

—HEIDI S.

spring

THERE ARE A MILLION FISH IN THE SEA... Don't commit to one guy before testing new waters... Have fun—play the field before settling down... I've heard it all over the last six years of dating my first love, Matt. We met my senior year of high school, and though I understood the concerns of committing to the only guy I have seriously dated, I decided to let the relationship take its natural course. Now we are engaged and I couldn't be happier. I think my relationship may intimidate or surprise some people, but sometimes a girl just finds her soul mate the first time around. —MELISSA K.

Shortly after turning 18, my parents made the decision to move. I hated the idea, but chose to go with them. Still, I was lonely, so I got a job at a candle factory to pass the time and make some college money. That first day, I saw him. His eyes were sky blue and huge dimples framed his smile. From then on, each time he passed, I'd say "Marry me!" loud enough for my coworkers to hear. After a few weeks of this, my coworker stopped him as he went by and said, "Enough already! Will you please marry her so she will be quiet?" That afternoon, he asked me out; five months later we were engaged, and a year later, we married. Not only did I gain a lifelong partner— ten years and counting—but I learned that sometimes the best things in life often come when you least expect them. —SARAH L.

two

Summer

Meeting you was fate.
Becoming your friend was a choice.
Falling in love with you was beyond my control.
Becoming your wife was my fairy tale come true.

before we met, we were two random people making every decision for the sole purpose and goal of meeting each other. Every breath led to us finding each other. Now, every breath leads us on to finding our future together.

Marriage is three parts love and seven parts forgiveness of sins.

—LAO TZU

When there is love in a marriage, there is harmony
in the home; when there is harmony in the home,
there is contentment in the community;
when there is contentment in the community, there is
prosperity in the nation; when there is prosperity
in the nation, there is peace in the world.

—CHINESE PROVERB

THOUGH MY HUSBAND *and I had lived together for some time, we never mentioned marriage. But when I became pregnant with our son, we began discussing the idea and even went as far as to look at rings. Still, there was no commitment. Nine months flew by, and after 15 grueling hours of labor, our son was born. With our new baby in my arms, my husband came into the hospital room, got down on one knee, and asked me to marry him. Having a child bonds two people together for life, but today, as a happily married couple, we also know that the birth of our son bonded us in so many more ways than just genetics.* —TABITHA F.

Perhaps friendship is
the process of my leading you
gently back to yourself.

—ANTOINE DE SAINT-EXUPERY

You'll always be my hero
because when it's good, it's very,
very good. And when it's bad,
I still have no doubts that
I love you!

For all the good times
And all the bad
We've held together
With all that we had.
The past is history
The present is now.
I'll love you forever
And stay true to my vows!

_I not only love you,
but love that you love me._

Friendship often ends in love;
but love in friendship—never.

— CHARLES CALEB COLTON

Building a Marriage to Last

There is more than one path to a perfect marriage,
but researchers have found that marriages strong enough to go
the distance share common characteristics. These include:

✻ Trusting and confiding in one another

✻ A willingness to lower expectations set before marriage

✻ Persistence over commitment: the willingness to pursue happiness
within the marriage rather than simply staying because of the commitment

✻ Respecting and valuing each other

✻ Expressing feelings to one another

✻ Intimacy and closeness

✻ Mutual sexual satisfaction

✻ Expressions of understanding and support

✻ Encouraging independence in one another

✻ Expressions of contentment and appreciation

Love me when I least deserve it, because
that's when I really need it.

—SWEDISH PROVERB

We've backpacked across Australia, lived out of a tent in
Tahiti, and took a nine-month trek across North America, Alaska,
and Canada. We've braved a grizzly attack and got married on our
mountain bikes in the mountains of the Cleveland National Forest.
But hands down, love has been the biggest adventure of them all!

Ask me to show you what love is and I'll show you my husband... There aren't many men who would graciously spend their honeymoon at a workshop put together by an online mosaic group, but that's exactly what he did. And on top of that, he enjoyed it (or, as a good husband, said that he did!).

It had been a horrible day, but as I headed out the door, my mom came up behind me, gave me a warm hug, and said, "When the going gets tough, remember: your mother loves you."

—CHELSEA R.

To get the full value of joy
you must have someone
to divide it with.

—MARK TWAIN

Honey, I knew from the moment you almost hit me
with your truck that we were meant to be. I love you
and every day we get to spend together.

fall

Perfectly imperfect is all one
ever needs to be worthy of love.

— KIM P.

I can't even begin to tell you
why some angels don't have wings.
But I know that it's true
because you are here.

In addition to being my brother, Chris is my reality check. No matter how old we get, he knows—and I know—that at heart, we are still two kids from Our Lady of Perpetual Help.

—JIM McCANN

After my divorce, the thought of love really scared me. I knew that if I wanted to find love I had to let someone in, yet opening my heart meant running the risk of opening it to hurt. I started hanging out with a friend, then realized he was the type of companion I had always wanted. We were in sync and he made me feel special and important whether we were together or apart. We stayed on the phone for hours watching the Game Show Network—he on his end, me on mine. One night he shared a eulogy he had written for his father's funeral and I knew I had found my future.

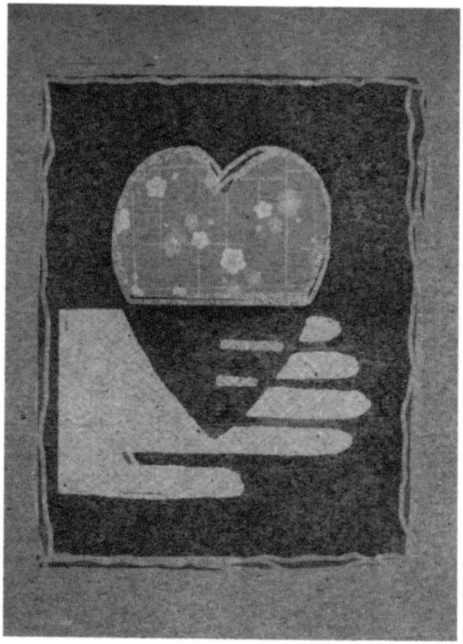

Well, life happened, and we were prevented from moving ahead, but I have a lot of nice moments to look back on, and I know now that I have a soul mate. More importantly, I learned that I am able to love again, physically, emotionally, and mentally. —HEIDI S.

Marriage takes commitment, forgiveness,
and unconditional love purified in the fire of
difficult times to become "silver love."

—LINDY A.

*One word frees us of all the weight and
pain of life: That word is* Love.

—SOPHOCLES

Love is not a need but an ecstasy . . .
a heart inflamed, a soul enchanted.

Oh, *the* comfort, the inexpressible comfort of feeling safe with a person, having neither to weigh thoughts nor measure words but to pour them all out, just as it is, chaff and grain together, knowing that a faithful hand will take and sift them, keeping what is worth keeping, and then, with the breath of kindness, blow the rest away. —GEORGE ELIOT

f there is one thing I learned about being a military brat, it's that infatuation may go on vacation, but true love never truly packs up and moves on. For years we moved around, landing in England when I was 12. It was there that I met Diane, my best friend, and Vincent, my first true love. As luck would have it, we transferred back to the states and I lost touch with them both. Still, I often wondered about them and whether I was the only one who felt such a strong connection to the people and place of that time.

Over the years, we all got married, raised families, and lived our lives, but with the miracle of the Internet, we began to reconnect. My friendship with Diane picked up right where it had left off and today, we're best friends, seeing each other at least once a year. Vincent and I, both divorced, also reconnected, discovering that our love for each other never died. So here we are, 35 years later, planning a wedding, happy to be part of a love that has come full circle. —KELLY D.

The world may take you
beautiful places but love is the
only way to travel.

—HEIDI K.

From you, I've learned that it's not about doing
extraordinary things, but doing ordinary things
with extraordinary love.

When I was 50, I went on a summer-long retreat to the country to write a book. In the late afternoons, I started taking long walks, trying to figure out the next step in my life. As the end of my stay approached, I began to sense the presence of a man while I was walking. Each day, the details became clearer—he was bald, solidly built. And I kept getting the message: You'll turn around and he'll be there. Was I going crazy, I wondered?

A couple months later, after I had returned to the city, I attended a class reunion. As I was walking in, I heard someone behind me. I turned around and there he was—the man that had come to me on my long walks. We immediately fell into such deep conversation that we didn't realize the room had filled with other classmates. Four hours later, he offhandedly said that now that we had met, perhaps he shouldn't move from New York, as he was in the process of doing.

"I have to be careful," I said. "I tend to rush these things."

"You too?" he responded. "I already have us married and living in the Berkshires."

Six weeks later, we moved there together; we were married on the lawn of the Williamsville Inn the following September. Twenty years later, we are still living happily ever after. —STEPHANIE O.

He wanted to marry me. He had a twinkle
in his eyes and a contagious laugh. He was compassionate,
fun, and adventurous. He loved me unconditionally. And
I knew I loved him.

But I was scared. How could I possibly know for certain
that he was the "right one," a man with whom I could
spend the rest of my life?

Now, after 28 years together, I can safely say that I don't
know if anyone truly knows the answer. It takes faith, a
deep trust in destiny, to make the leap. But when you're
willing to risk it all, you could end up as lucky as me . . .
eight beautiful children, a friendship stretching three decades,
and someone with whom to share everyday sorrows and
joys, someone to love. —DIXIE C.

"I Love You" Around the World

Armenian—**Yes kez sirumem**

Cambodian—Soro lahn nhee ah

Mandarin—**Wo ai ni** French—Je t'aime, Je t'adore

German—**Ich liebe dich** Hawaiian—**Aloha Au Ia `oe**

Hindi—Hum Tumhe Pyar Karte hae Italian—**Ti amo**

Japanese—Aishiteru or Anata ga daisuki desu

Moroccan—Ana moajaba bik Spanish—**Te quiero/Te amo**

Tahitian—**Ua Here Vau Ia Oe** Turkish—Seni Seviyorum

Yiddish—**Ikh hob dikh**

Love is more than a feeling.
It is something "you" do each and
every day. Thank you.

AS A PALM READER, I was working at the Colorado State Fair when an elderly gentleman sat down and asked me to read his palm.

"Do you have any issues?" I asked.

"No," he said, but he did have a love story he wanted me to unravel from his palm. "I want to see if you are truly psychic," he said.

Immediately, I saw his first love, but no marriage. He agreed, telling me he was in love, but the woman turned him down because he was leaving soon for the service. It was during World War II.

"All the time I was flying over Guadalcanal, I thought about her," he said. "I had her picture on a chain around my neck throughout the war. When I came back home, she had married someone else. But I never forgot her."

Next, I saw him married. It was a long marriage—forty years, and that only recently, he had become a widow.

"You're right again," he said. "Do you see anything else?"

I did—his old flame. I told him something wonderful was about to happen to them both. He beamed.

After her husband died, she tracked him down using a lead from a high school alumni newsletter.

"Somehow, I got invited to her house, and darned if I didn't hop a plane the next day. We spent a week together and rekindled our love. Toward the end of my stay, we were out shopping. She strolled into a dress shop; I went next door to the jeweler and asked to see engagement rings. Just as he pulled out several trays, she walked in. I proposed then and there.

"She cried. I cried. The storeowner and sales clerks cried. They took our picture to use in their ads.

"I asked her to choose whatever ring she liked, but she pushed the more expensive solitaires aside.

"'It has to be this one,' she said, pointing to a simple ring with four tiny diamonds. 'I must have this one because it represents the four decades we missed being together.'" —MYRNA G.

So often you hear about the grand gestures of love:

the proposals on the top of the Eiffel Tower,

the dozen roses delivered to work, the jewelry and

dinners. All of these are wonderful things . . .

but they are not love. Love is found in the little

gestures: the smile I see when I open my eyes every

morning, the effort you make to care for our baby

and let me get extra sleep, the herb garden you

planted because you knew I wanted one but didn't

have the time to do it myself. I was looking for love

in a big way and found it in the every day.

Love is so much better the second time around — even if it is with my first wife! Silly as it sounds, my wife and I were married for seven years before divorcing. After a lot of growing up on both of our parts, we remarried seven years later, picking up right where we left off. This time around, there are still "speed bumps" in our marriage. There are issues that continue to pop up. But the second time around, we have learned to respond differently. We know that one fight doesn't make or break a marriage as long as we are both committed for the long haul. We know that the embers continue to glow even when the fire has died down. Maybe that's what mature love is. —BARRY C.

four

winter

The more I think it over,
the more I feel that there is nothing more
truly artistic than to love people.

— VINCENT VAN GOGH

I have been in love with my husband for 25 years, so
long that sometimes I ask myself, "Can this be real?"
Then he says, "I would marry you all over again!,"
and I know that yes, this is real love. — BJR

Eternity exists because of the
eternal love you have given me.
Let's explore life's best together
as we continue to become one
with each other, as we continue
to grow and love.

At age 42, I suddenly found myself a single mother of five children. Larry was 52 . . . an only child, never married, with as much time to travel, golf, and ski as he wanted. We met at a convention where we were both speaking, then began dating long distance. One day, after we had been together a while, he commented, "You know, sharks have to keep moving forward or they die." I burst out crying, thinking he was telling me he wanted to move on. As it turned out, he was proposing—he was ready to take our relationship forward into marriage. And he even agreed to move from Denver to Kansas City. He didn't want the children's lives to be upset, he said.

A month before our wedding, my youngest daughter was in a horrific accident and broke her neck. I called Larry from the emergency room and told him he had time to back out, that it was one thing to take on a woman with five children, but quite another thing to ask of someone if one of them was paralyzed. "What do you think marriage is all about?" he asked. As it turned out, my daughter survived, and Larry's expertise as a physical therapist helped her get through it. After sixteen years, I am a believer that true love is possible no matter the age or circumstances. —CATHY S.

One Valentine's Day, we got a call from a World War II veteran. Like millions of other kids in the forties, he went off to war with the memory of his prom date, a pretty girl from his hometown. But four years of war change a lot of things, and when the soldier came back, he had his sights set on a life outside his little New Hampshire village.

Time went by. The soldier married and raised a family. When he was older, he lost his wife. He called us because he had never forgotten that young girl from his youth. "Could you find her?" he asked. This is exactly the kind of challenge our customer service reps like to take on. A rep hopped on the case; one phone call led to another, and finally, we found a recently widowed woman in the same small town.

The old soldier sent her a corsage that was a duplicate of the one that he had given her at the prom all those years ago. The card read, "If you're the May Anne that I left in '41, I'd sure like to get caught up with you." She was. He did. And fittingly, 1-800-FLOWERS got the order for their wedding flowers. —JIM McCANN

When I look into the life we share, I imagine all that we could
have been individually. Then I see what we have created together.
There is no greater life than a life shared with you.

HOLDING CLOSE
WITHOUT SMOTHERING . . .
BREAKING OUT
WITHOUT BREAKING UP.

Love is no assignment for cowards.

—OVID

because I am a survivor of child abuse, marriage has never been easy for me—or my husband. But over the past 25 years that we have been married, he has shown me unconditional love. Joel held my hand through ten years of extremely difficult healing, and he has loved me without question when I have acted in unlovely ways. Through it all, he was somehow able to perceive who I was intended to be before the abuse, and his unwavering faith in me and our relationship has helped me become the woman I am today. Having the honor of walking through life with one person all these years has meant walking through the fire at times, but in doing so, all things selfish and hurtful have burned away, leaving only a deep and abiding love for each other. —LINDY A.

A friend loves at all times.

— PROVERBS 17:17

*How can I express in one sentence what
a lifetime with you has meant to me?*

Dear George,
Remember no man is a failure
who has friends.
Thanks for the wings!
Love, Clarence

—CLARENCE, *IT'S A WONDERFUL LIFE*

Seven years ago, my family moved next door to Mr. Paul and Mrs. Agnes. An elderly couple, the two were spunky and fun-loving. They went to lunch and dinner together almost daily, and it was obvious they enjoyed each other's company even if they were doing something as simple as sitting outside watching my children play in our backyard.

We didn't know then, but Mrs. Agnes was already very sick, and eventually, she could no longer get out of bed. One day, Mr. Paul came outside and clipped a bouquet of gorgeous pink roses from their backyard. I watched, crying, as he put them into water and took them to her bedside. A few weeks later, she died. At her funeral, the casket was covered with a huge arrangement of pink flowers. Our entire family cried.

Since Mrs. Agnes' death, Mr. Paul still goes to lunch, but looks so lonely without the love of his life by his side. Not a day goes by without him talking of how much he misses his "Aggie." And just like before, he clips a bouquet of roses every few days. When I asked why, he said he still goes out for lunch and dinner, only he gets it to go. He then drives over to Aggie's grave where he eats and talks with her, and tells her how much he misses her. The roses, as always, are for Aggie. And of course, I cried. —BETH D.

I love you, my forgetful wife.
Who knew that love not only
lasts longer than memory,
but that it continues to grow?

*Y*ou name it . . . We've been through it: unemployment, disability, a long-distance relationship, relocation, death, teenagers, financial troubles, surgeries, family problems, and much deeper, more personal challenges. And yet when he looks into my eyes, my heart pounds. I get butterflies when he pulls into the drive. I melt when I hear his voice.

Over the years, we have had rough times and day-to-day obstacles, but I know in my heart, down to my toes, in my soul, that our everlasting love can withstand anything life throws at us . . . and despite what's going on around us, it will be an amazing journey because we are in this together. —MARIESA S.

Love means giving in
without giving up...

SOMETIMES LOVE DOESN'T WORK OUT, even when you give it everything you have. Sometimes you have to let go because it's best for both of you. Sometimes it hurts. But it's not life-ending. It can be a second chance. You are given an opportunity to start over. Start fresh. Dream big, then dream bigger. In the end, you may be surprised by the peace that comes from realizing that by breaking, you can grow even stronger. —MAURA B.

In the Victorian era, lovers would send each other secret messages using floriography, the language of flowers. Today, a bouquet of flowers is synonymous with caring thoughts, but you can sneak in a secret code by choosing specific flowers to give.

Red Carnation 🌹 My heart aches for you.

Daffodil 🌹 Unrequited Love

Purple Lilac 🌹 First emotion of love

Orange Lily 🌹 Passion, desire

Orchid 🌹 Refined beauty

White Rose 🌹 Eternal love

Yellow Rose 🌹 Friendship

Sunflower 🌹 Pure and lofty thoughts

Red Tulip 🌹 Declaration of love

It's not the marriage I expected, but when we said "in sickness and in health," we meant it. In the first year of our marriage, my husband became ill with a physically and mentally disabling disease. I've cared for him for 11 years, and through God's loving grace, our love for each other has continued to grow. My husband can do little for himself, but I find comfort in the touch of his hands. I am uplifted by his quiet presence. And though he talks very little, his whispered "I love yous" leave me overwhelmed. —TERRI C

Grow old along with me!
The best is yet to be,
the last of life,
for which the first was made.

—ROBERT BROWNING

illustration credits

l le promet, croyez-le, fût-ce un jour.

ne mourrait—? la vie est dans l'amour

, Avec ses feux je peignais ses douleurs:

ue cette image en paraît moins charmante.

au milieu de mes larmes, C'était l'amour

e ciel... qu'avec lui j'ai perdu.

e; Il brûle tout, ce doux empoisonneur.

Demandez donc s'il donne le bonheur:

De gré, de force, amour sera le maître;

vous souffrirez, ou vous ferez souffrir.

Dès qu'il revient, on tremble nuit et jour

Cependant...oui, l'amour rend heureuse!

Vous demandez si l'amour rend heureuse

Ah! pour un jour d'existence amoureuse, Q

Quand je vivais tendre et craintive ama

Sur son portrait j'ai versé tant de pleurs,

Si le sourire, éclair inattendu, Brille parf

c'était lui, mais sans armes; c'éta

Sans lui, le cœur est un foyer sans flam

J'ai dit bien vrai comme il déchire une â

Vous le saurez: oui, quoi qu'il en puisse

Et, dans sa fièvre alors lente à guérir,

Dès qu'on l'a vu, son absence est affreu

Souvent enfin la mort est dans l'amour.